AF334131

HEART BEATS
Songs without Music

lyrics by Fred Kolo

COLUMBINE PRESS
East Hampton NY

TO *.*.*.

for opening a couple of windows,
turning on a light.

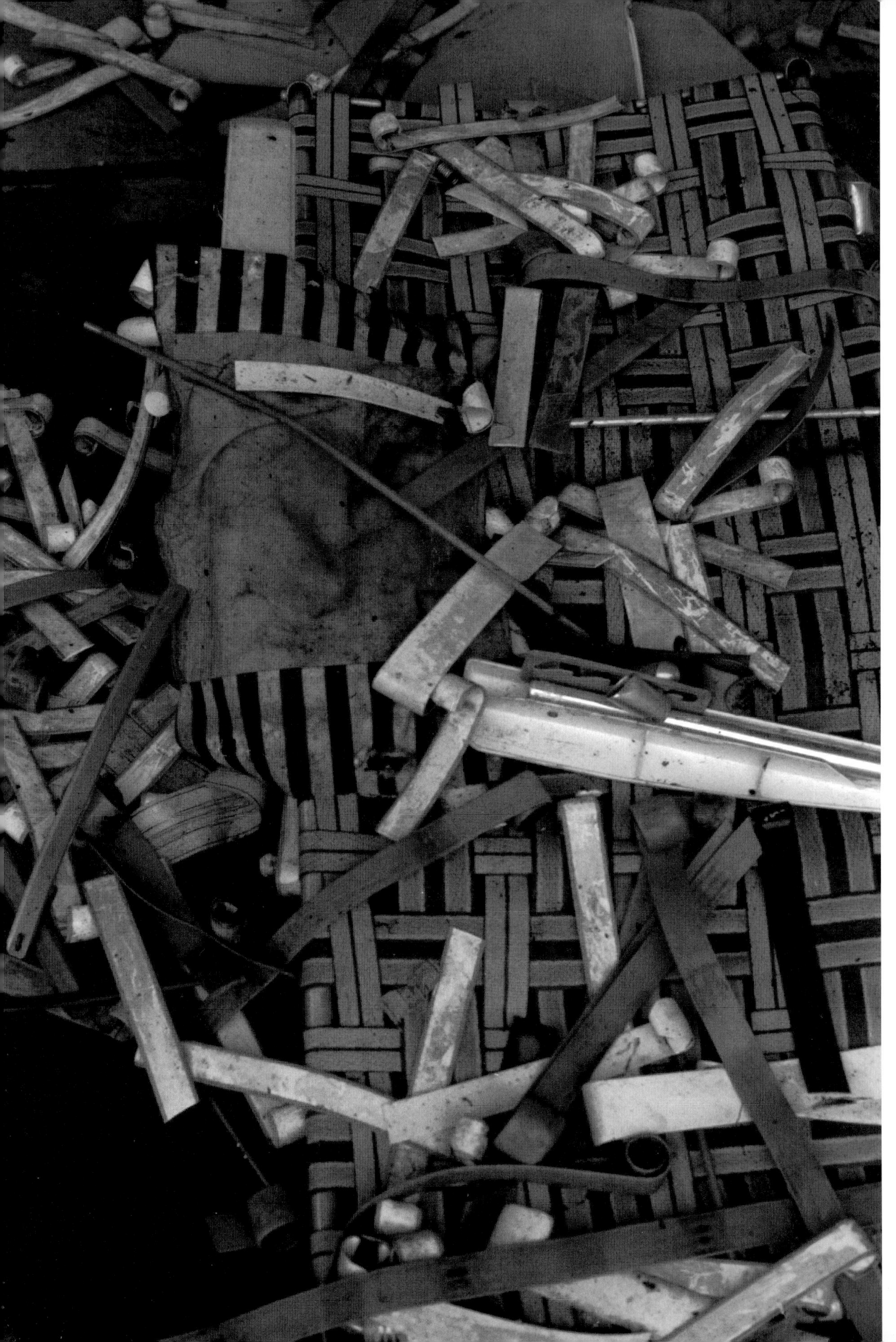

DAY OF WRATH

I'VE BEEN WARDEN OF THIS PRISON
FOR CLOSE TO FORTY YEARS.
THE SPECTER OF ITS CRIMES
NO LONGER BRINGS ME TEARS.
I'VE HARDENED MY HEART
BUT KEPT APART
FROM THE WORLD OUTSIDE,
WHERE ONLY VICTIMS RESIDE.
COME AND TAKE A TOUR WITH ME,
IF YOU HAVE A STOMACH THAT CAN ENDURE THE SEA.

IN THE FIRST CELL IS LYDA, THE CARNIVAL QUEEN.
SHE WAS A GREAT BEAUTY WHO GOT PRETTY MEAN,
BUT THE SCARS ON HER THIGHS AND ONE BREAST
ATTEST TO SOME MISTREATMENT,
SO PERHAPS SHE HAD A REASON,
BUT SHE BROUGHT A NEW HORROR TO THE HOLIDAY SEASON.

THE McGONIGLE TWINS IN CELL NUMBER FIVE
HAD SOME TROUBLE KEEPING THEIR LOVERS ALIVE.
THEY'D PERFECTED THEIR DANCING
WITH A GREAT DEAL OF PRACTICE.
THE SENSUOUS TANGLE OF FOUR ARMS, FOUR LEGS, AND FOUR BREASTS
WAS A MAJOR ATTRACTION,
DROVE MEN TO DISTRACTION;
BUT YOU COULD LOSE YOUR HEAD,
OR YOUR LIMBS,
TO THE PRETTY, IDENTICAL McGONIGLE TWINS.

CELL SEVENTEEN IS TEDDY THE TUNER.
HE SINGS AND HE DANCES WITH MARVELOUS STYLE,
BUT THE BLACK LEATHER TAP SHOES HE MOVES WITH SUCH SPEED
HAVE SHARP LITTLE RAZORS THAT CAN CAUSE ONE TO BLEED
SHOULD ONE BE SO IMPRUDENT
AS TO SMILE IN HIS DIRECTION
OR TO TAKE A FURTIVE GLANCE
AT HIS CONSTANT, IF RATHER SMALL, ERECTION.

SHUFFLE, STEP, SHUFFLE, STEP, SHUFFLE, SHUFFLE, SHUFFLE, CUT.
SHUFFLE, STEP, SHUFFLE, CUT, SHUFFLE, CUT, SHUFFLE, CUT, CUT, CUT.

HIS FEET MOVED AT AN ASTONISHING CLIP;
THE SMILE ON HIS FACE WOULD NEVER SLIP.
HIS SPECIALTY NUMBER FEATURED A FLOOR
GENEROUSLY SPRINKLED WITH SALT,
AND IF THE DANCE DIDN'T LAST VERY LONG,
WELL, IT WASN'T YOUR FAULT.

continued

DAY OF WRATH continued

CELL TWENTY-FOUR IS A KIND OF A DORM
"THE BOYS IN THE BACK SEAT," ALL EIGHT.
THEIR PRIOR BEHAVIOR PARTED FROM THE NORM;
IN A LITTLE TIN TOWN, NO ONE WENT OUT LATE.

MANY A WOMAN AND MANY A GIRL
LEARNED THROUGH HER TEARS ABOUT PAIN.
THE BOYS ALL LINED UP IN AN ORDERLY FASHION
AND IF ONE MISSED OUT
THROUGH UNCONSCIOUSNESS OR, YES, EVEN DEATH,
HE NEVER COMPLAINED.
TOMORROW WAS,
AS THE LADY IN WHITE IN THEIR FAVORITE MOVIE USED TO SAY,
ANOTHER DAY.

SHOULD THEY ESCAPE, WHICH ISN'T UNLIKELY,
YOU DON'T NEED TO LOCK UP YOUR DAUGHTERS AND WIVES.
IN THE SIX YEARS SINCE THEY'VE BEEN PUT AWAY
"THE BOYS IN THE BACK SEAT" HAVE ALL BECOME GAY.
EXCEPT, PERHAPS, LITTLE MAX
WHO MAY SOMEDAY,
THOUGH HIS ETHICS WERE ALWAYS RATHER LOOSE,
SEEK REVENGE FOR SEVERAL YEARS OF QUIETLY-ENDURED ABUSE.

LITTLE EMMA IN TWENTY-EIGHT STILL LOOKS LIKE A CHILD,
THOUGH SHE BEGAN HER TRADE AT THE AGE OF THIRTEEN.
REALLY HER BEHAVIOR WAS ALWAYS RATHER MILD:
LIKE THE REAL LIVE TOY SHE SOMETIMES SEEMED,
SHE WAS NEVER MOODY, NEVER MEAN.
THE ONLY THING THAT WAS RATHER QUEER
WAS HER PASSION TO KEEP JUST A SMALL SOUVENIR.

IN FORTY-EIGHT IS HENRY, A DAPPER GENT
WITH A LITERARY BENT.
HE WAS RETIRING AND RATHER SCHOLARLY,
COULDN'T STAND BORES,
AND WAS FREQUENTLY SEEN IN SECOND HAND STORES.

HE BOUGHT FIRST EDITIONS AND AUTOGRAPHED COPIES,
OLD PRINTS AND LITHOGRAPHS AND ETCHINGS OF POPPIES;
READ COLERIDGE AND BYRON AND THE MARQUIS DE SADE,
ARGUED WITH CLERKS ABOUT THE EXISTENCE OF GOD.
SOMETIMES HIS CANE WAS COVERED WITH LARD
AND HE REVERED ABOVE ALL THE WORDS OF THE BARD.

HIS MORE PRIVATE ENCOUNTERS WENT OFTEN ASTRAY;
JUST WHAT WENT WRONG WAS NOT EASY TO SAY,
BUT HE LEFT ON THE BUREAU A SMALL BAG OF VINYL MESH
CONTAINING JUST A POUND OF FLESH.
OF BLOOD, NOT ONE DROP;
NOT EVEN THE CORONER, WHO'S BEEN ABOUT,
COULD FIGURE THAT ONE OUT.

THERE'VE BEEN CRIMES AGAINST WOMEN
AND CRIMES AGAINST MEN,
CRIMES AGAINST CHILDREN AND CRIMES AGAINST DOGS.
IF YOU'VE LOST A CAT, LOOK TO LISA IN TEN,
WHILE HERMAN, IN SEVEN, HAS BUTCHERED SOME HOGS.

SOMEDAY THE WALLS OF THIS PRISON WILL CRUMBLE,
THE DOORS WILL FLY OPEN AS LIGHT FILLS THE SKY;
IN THUNDER AND LIGHTNING THE TOWERS WILL TUMBLE;
THIRTY FLAMING CHARIOTS WILL SLOWLY RIDE BY.

LYDA AND LISA AND ALL OF THE BOYS,
HERMAN AND HENRY, EMMA WITH HER TOYS,
THE TWINS AND THE TUNER, ALL WILL LINE UP,
RAISE A CUP, DRINK IN THE NOISE,
THEN MARCH TO THEIR MAKER
FOR THE FINAL JUDGMENT DAY.

WHAT WILL HE SAY?

WHEN HE LOOKS IN THOSE EYES
WILL HE DESPISE THE COLDNESS THERE?
WILL HE LASH OUT AND CONDEMN THEM TO BURN,
TO TAKE THE PUNISHMENT THEY WORKED SO HARD TO EARN?

OR WILL HE SHUDDER IN SORROW
AND WONDER WHO MADE THEM?
ALL OF THOSE HEARTS LACKING EMOTION,
WHERE DID THEY COME FROM,
WHAT HAD GONE WRONG?
WHERE WAS THE SONG HE INTENDED
WHEN PEN WAS SET TO PAGE?
WILL GOD BEGIN TO RAGE?
OR QUIETLY WEEP AS HE CUTS HIS VEINS
AND GOES TO SLEEP?

morning

COLD AND HEAT

I CALLED YOU WAY TOO LATE LAST NIGHT;
PERHAPS YOU WEREN'T ALONE.
YOUR VOICE WAS COLD AND DISTANT;
I SHOULDN'T HAVE TOUCHED THE PHONE.
I'VE BEEN A BIT INSISTANT
AND OVERLY PERSISTANT.
INSTEAD OF FANNING THE FIRE
OR GRADUALLY MAKING MY MARK,
I'VE BLOWN OUT THE SPARK.

COLD AND HEAT,
COLD AND HEAT,
HEARTS THAT NEVER MEET.
WE WILL PASS AS STRANGERS IN THE STREET.

IMAGINATION'S FANTASY
BECOMES A DIM REMEMBERED DREAM.
THE TANGLED SCHEME OF YOU AND ME
IS SORTED INTO SEPARATE STRANDS.
WE WILL NEVER JOIN OUR HANDS.

I SUPPOSE I'VE BEEN COMPULSIVE,
WAY BEYOND CONTROL.
MY PLAY FOR YOU WAS OUT OF BOUNDS,
NOT AT ALL DISCREET OR SMART,
BUT IF I'VE MADE MY BLUNDERS
THEY CAME DIRECTLY FROM MY HEART.

COLD AND HEAT,
COLD AND HEAT,
HEARTS THAT NEVER MEET.
WE WILL PASS AS STRANGERS IN THE STREET.

THE MILD APRIL DAYS WILL COME,
SNOW WILL MELT AND FIRES DIE,
STILL I'M HOPING THAT THE SMALLEST EMBER
WILL REMAIN IN MY HEART FOR NEXT DECEMBER.

COLD AND HEAT,
COLD AND HEAT,
HEARTS THAT NEVER MEET.
WE WILL PASS AS STRANGERS IN THE STREET.
COLD AND HEAT,
COLD AND HEAT.

POST-MODERN LOVE

I WAS BORN INTO A MODERN WORLD,
BUT TIME HAS A WAY OF MOVING FAST;
IT SEEMS THAT WHAT WAS MODERN
HAS NOW BECOME THE PAST.
I REMEMBER WITH REAL NOSTALGIA
THE AFFAIRS I USE TO SAVOR;
THE SPIRIT MOVED, THE BODY FOLLOWED,
NO MATTER WHAT THE FLAVOR;
BUT STORM CLOUDS COVERED UP BLUE SKY,
AND WHAT WAS MODERN HAS PASSED US BY:

LOVE HAS BECOME RISKY,
YOU KNOW WHAT THEY SAY;
IF YOU'RE FEELING PARTICULARLY FRISKY,
WELL, PUT THAT FEELING AWAY.
IF YOU HAVE A GOOD CONNECTION
FOR SOPHISTICATED PROTECTION
PERHAPS YOU CAN TAKE A CHANCE;
IF YOU HAVE SOME OBJECTS MADE OF LATEX,
AND RUBBER GLOVES BY PLATEX,
THEN YOU NEEDN'T SHY AWAY FROM ROMANCE.

POST-MODERN LOVE
POST-MODERN LOVE
IT QUIETS THE DOVE
THIS POST-MODERN LOVE

YOU NEED TO KNOW THE LOGISTICS,
AND HOW TO PLAY THE STATISTICS,
THOUGH ALL THIS PREPARATION
CAN SURELY LEAD TO DEFLATION.
THIS INHIBITION OF DESIRE
COULD PUT OUT ANY FIRE.

    POST-MODERN LOVE
    POST-MODERN LOVE
    IT SMOTHERS THE DOVE
    THIS POST-MODERN LOVE

AND NOW A NEW COMPLEXITY
IS ADDED TO CUPID'S MISSION:
BEFORE YOU CAN MAKE A ROMANTIC MOVE,
YOU HAVE TO ASK PERMISSON.
IN THESE TIMES YOUR FIRST LOVE
HAD BETTER BE YOUR LAST.
DON'T EVEN THINK OF HOLDING A HAND
UNTIL IT WEARS A WEDDING BAND.

    POST-MODERN LOVE
    POST-MODERN LOVE
    IT MURDERS THE DOVE
    THIS POST-MODERN LOVE

IT ONCE SEEMED IMPORTANT
TO KEEP UP WITH THE TIMES,
BUT WHAT USED TO BE SILVER DOLLARS
NOW ARE NICKLES AND DIMES.
I WAS BORN A MODERNIST
BUT IN THE FACE OF ALL THAT'S NEW
I MUST DESIST.
I'VE NOW BECOME A CLASSICIST.

JUNK

YOU GAVE ME THAT OLD CHEVROLET
IT'S SITTING IN THE YARD
I GUESS I SAID IT WAS NEAT
THAT DAY YOU DROVE IT DOWN MY STREET

YOU GAVE ME THAT BOOK OF POEMS
THEY'RE SITTING ON THE SHELF
WHEN YOU READ ME THAT ONE ABOUT THE NIGHT
I LIKED IT ALL RIGHT

YOU GAVE ME THAT OLD T.V.
IT'S SITTING IN THE ATTIC
I KNOW, I SAID IT HAD BEEN YEARS
SINCE I'D SEEN RABBIT EARS

YOU GAVE ME THAT ROTARY TELEPHONE
IT'S UNDERNEATH THE STAIRS
JUST 'CAUSE I MADE YOU SMILE
WHEN I TOLD YOU THERE'S NO NAME
        FOR THE LITTLE THING THAT
            STOPS YOUR FINGER WHEN YOU DIAL

YOU GAVE ME THAT COOKIE JAR
SHAPED LIKE A VALENTINE
YOU FILLED IT WITH CHOC'LATE CANDIES
THAT TASTED JUST LIKE TURPENTINE

YOU GAVE ME THAT OLD RUG
YOU SAID IT WAS ORIENTAL
I FIGURED IT WAS A SIGN
YOU WERE GETTING SENTIMENTAL

YOU GAVE ME A RADIO AND A KITCHEN SINK
AN OLD FUR COAT YOU SAID WAS MINK
I COULDN'T SELL AND BANK IT
AND IT'S NOT A VERY GOOD BLANKET

I'M SURE YOUR GRANDFATHER'S TUXEDO
MEANT A LOT TO HIM
THE LITTLE HIP FLASK
STILL WAS FULL OF GIN

THE OLD PORCH SWING
THE GIANT BALL OF STRING
THE WARING BLENDER AND THE TOASTER
THE ANGORA SWEATER AND THE TURKEY ROASTER
OF ALL THE THINGS YOU GAVE TO ME
THERE'S NOTHING THAT I'D CHOOSE.
ARE YOU JUST DUMPING ON ME
THE STUFF THAT YOU CAN'T USE?
OR IS IT REAL EMOTION
THAT CAUSES THIS COMMOTION?
IF SO, I'LL DO MY PART,
BUT, BABY,
THERE'S A JUNK YARD IN YOUR HEART.

EXIT
IN
NO
LIFEGUARDS
ON DUTY
L.I.S.PR+H.P.C.

THANKS

AT LAST YOU'VE GONE.
I KNOW I'LL CARRY ON;
TAKE MY HEART BACK OFF THE SHELF,
START FEELING GOOD ABOUT MYSELF.
MEMORIES?
I'VE GOT A FEW.
THERE ARE PLENTY OF THINGS I WON'T FORGET.
AT LEAST NOT YET.
YOU MAY NOT LIKE MY ATTITUDE.
WOULD YOU PREFER SOME GRATITUDE?

THANKS FOR THE PLASTIC CHRISTMAS TREE
THANKS FOR THE TRIP TO TENNESSEE
THANKS FOR THE DAY AT EPCOT CENTER
THANKS FOR BEING MY TORMENTOR

THANKS FOR THE WEIGHT GAIN
THANKS FOR THE PAIN
THANKS FOR THE SLEEPLESS NIGHTS
THANKS FOR THE BITTER FIGHTS

THANKS FOR THE TAPE OF TAMMY WYNETTE
THANKS FOR THE GAME OF RUSSIAN ROULETTE
THANKS FOR THAT ARIZONA SUNSET
THANKS FOR A LIFE OF TOTAL REGRET

THANKS FOR THE TEMPER YOU SOMETIMES SUPPRESSED
THANKS FOR LEAVING ME TOTALLY DEPRESSED
THANKS FOR NEVER KNOWING WHEN YOU'D REAPPEAR
THANKS FOR THAT BITTER LITTLE SOUVENIR

THANKS FOR THE CONFESSION
THANKS FOR THE REPRESSION
THANKS FOR ZERO-BALANCE BANKING
THANKS FOR THE SPANKING
FOR THE YAPPING AND THE SCRAPPING AND THE SLAPPING
FOR THE NIGHTS THAT WERE ENDLESS
FOR LEAVING ME TOTALLY FRIENDLESS
THANKS FOR BEING MY AGGRESSOR
THANKS FOR BEING MY OPPRESSER

THE HOLE IN THE WALL
THE CRACK IN THE SINK
THE BROKEN SOFA LEG
THE FOURTEENTH DRINK
I CAN GIVE YOU ALL OF THESE
THANK YOU FOR THE MEMORIES.

PARK
CLOSES AT
SUNSET
· CLOSED ·

JULY 4, 1995

MISSED THE FIREWORKS THIS YEAR;
MISSED THE ROCKETS IN THE SKY;
MISSED THE BURGERS AND THE BEANS;
MISSED THE COKES AND APPLE PIE.

THE DAY WAS CLEAR;
THE SEA WAS CALMER THAN A POND;
THE SUN SCREAMED WITH LIGHT,
SCREAMED JUST LIKE OUR FIGHT,
SLAMMED INTO THE EARTH
JUST LIKE THE DOOR LAST NIGHT.

WE CELEBRATE OUR INDEPENDENCE,
THE BIRTH OF LIBERTY.
WELL, YOU DID IT FOR ME:
YOU MADE ME FREE.

I'LL BE A REAL AMERICAN,
OVERFED AND KIND OF SAD,
CLING PATHETICALLY
TO EVERY FAD.
I'LL PRAISE THE FLAG,
RAISE MY VOICE.
"LIVE FREE OR DIE", THEY SAY.
IS THAT THE ONLY CHOICE?

DID THEY KNOW,
TWO HUNDRED YEARS AGO,
THE PRICE:
THE BEAUTY OF THIS LAND,
THE PRECIOUS GIFT,
THE LIFE ALONE,
THE QUIET MOAN?

FREEDOM HAS BEGUN;
MY LIFE WITH YOU HAS ENDED.
GUESS I'LL GO ON;
PROBABLY WON'T CRY;
BUT SOMEDAY
LET ME DIE
ON THE FOURTH OF JULY.

noon

RX

YOU KNOW I LIKE YOU
BUT I NEED A LITTLE SPACE,
NEED TO SPEND SOME TIME
IN A COMPLETELY DIFFERENT PLACE.
I BARELY SAID GOODBYE.
I HOPED YOU'D UNDERSTAND.
I SAW YOU IN THE REAR VIEW MIRROR
STANDING BY THE GATE
AS I DROVE AWAY TO A DIFFERENT STATE.
SPENT A FEW DAYS WITH A COUPLE OF FRIENDS,
BUT THAT'S NOT WHERE THE MATTER ENDS.

I WAS FEELING OUT OF SORTS,
KIND OF DISCOMBOBULATED.
I WENT TO SEE A DOCTOR.
I HOPED TO GET SEDATED.
IN MEDICAL MATTERS
I MAY NOT BE VERY SMART,
BUT I TOLD HIM I WAS PRETTY SURE
SOMETHIN' WAS HAPP'NIN' WITH MY HEART.

FIRST HE POKED AND PROBED A LOT
AND FELT MY BACK AND HAND,
HE SHOOK HIS HEAD AND MUTTERED SOMETHING
I COULDN'T UNDERSTAND.
THEN HE HAD ME BREATHE AND COUGH
AND FILL A JAR WITH PISS.
HE LOOKED ME IN THE EYE AND SAID,
"SON, I NEVER SEEN A CASE LIKE THIS."

"YOU'VE GOT PALPITATIONS
AND FIBRILLATIONS.
THIS COULD BE SOMETHING PRETTY BIG.
TRY STAYING HOME,
SPEND SOME TIME ALONE.
YOUR HEART'S DOIN' A KIND OF A JIG.
CALL ME IF IT DOESN'T EASE.
THAT'LL BE FIFTY DOLLARS, PLEASE."

continued

I TRIED TO RELAX AND SETTLE DOWN
BUT MY HEART WAS REALLY GOIN' TO TOWN.
I WENT RIGHT BACK TO SEE THE DOC.
BY NOW I WAS IN A STATE OF SHOCK.
HE PUT ALL MY SYMPTOMS ON A GREAT BIG LIST,
AND SAID HE BETTER GET ME TO A SPECIALIST.
"HE'LL FIX YOU UP IF YOU CAN AFFORD HIS FEES.
THAT'LL BE FIFTY DOLLARS, PLEASE."

"YOU'VE GOT PALPITATIONS
AND FIBRILLATIONS.
YOUR HEART'S DOIN' A KIND OF A JIG.
GO TO SOMEONE REALLY SMART,
WHO SPECIALIZES IN THE HEART.
THIS COULD BE SOMETHING PRETTY BIG."

NOW DOCS WHO SPECIALIZE
IN MATTERS OF THE HEART
CAN USUALLY TELL WHAT'S WRONG
JUST BY LOOKIN' AT YOUR CHART;
BUT WHEN I SAW THE FROWN ON HIS FACE
I FIGURED I WAS A MORE DIFFICULT CASE.
HE PUT ME IN A BIG MACHINE.
WITH PADS AND WIRES IT WAS ALL PRETTY MEAN,
BUT UP ON THE WALL IN A LIGHT KIND OF GREEN
THERE WAS MY HEART ON A T.V. SCREEN.

YOU COULD SEE PALPITATIONS
AND FIBRILLATIONS,
MY HEART DID A KIND OF A JIG.
IN THE LIGHT KIND OF GREEN
ON THAT T.V. SCREEN
THIS LOOKED LIKE SOMETHING PRETTY BIG.

"SON, I'M THE BEST MAN IN THE BUSINESS
AND I'VE GOT SOME LITTLE TRICKS.
YOU'VE GOT A PROBLEM WITH YOUR HEART
THAT ONLY I CAN FIX.
I DON'T KNOW HOW IT HAPPENED
BUT YOU BROKE YOUR HEART IN TWO.
I CAN PUT IT BACK TOGETHER
WITH A LITTLE CRAZY GLUE.
WE CAN DO IT RIGHT NOW
OR TOMORROW IF YOU PLEASE.
DON'T WORRY ABOUT THE COST,
IT'S ONLY TWENTY G'S."

"YOU'VE GOT PALPITATIONS
AND FIBRILLATIONS.
YOUR HEART'S DOIN' A KIND OF A JIG.
WE'LL GET YOU THROUGH
WITH A LITTLE CRAZY GLUE.
THIS COULD BE SOMETHING PRETTY BIG."

WELL, TWENTY G'S SEEMED LIKE QUITE A LOT,
SO I SAID "NO THANKS, IT'S MONEY I AIN'T GOT."
I FIGURED I SHOULDN'T BE ALONE,
THAT'S WHEN I CALLED YOU ON THE PHONE.
YOU WERE ALWAYS PRETTY SMART.
MAYBE YOU COULD FIX MY HEART.
YOU SAID "COME ON HOME, BRING YOUR HEART TO ME.
I'LL PUT IT BACK TOGETHER WITH SOME T.L.C."

NOW I GOT PALPITATIONS
AND FIBRILLATIONS.
MY HEART'S DOIN' A KIND OF A JIG.
I JUST NEVER KNEW
THAT THE TREATMENT WAS YOU.
AND THIS IS SOMETHING REALLY BIG.

GYPSY BOY

GYPSY BOY, GYPSY BOY,
HAIR SO BLACK, YOUR EYES
SO DARK AND SAD,
SO YOUNG TO BE SO WISE,
TO KNOW SO MUCH ABOUT GOOD AND BAD.

DID YOUR MAMA TELL YOUR FORTUNE
WHEN YOU WERE ONLY THREE?
HAVE YOU GROWN UP KNOWING
JUST WHAT LIFE WILL BE?

DO YOU KNOW ABOUT YOUR FIRST LOVE?
DO YOU KNOW ABOUT YOUR LAST?
DO YOU KNOW ABOUT THE HEARTACHES,
AND HOW LIFE MOVES SO FAST?

GYPSY BOY, GYPSY BOY,
WITH EYES SO SAD,
CAN YOU EVER BE HAPPY?
CAN YOU EVER BE GLAD?

WHEN YOU LOOKED INTO YOUR MAMA'S CRYSTAL BALL
DID YOU SEE IT ALL?
DO YOU KNOW IF YOU'LL GET OLD AND GREY,
OR DIE BEFORE THE END OF TODAY?
DO YOU KNOW WHEN HAPPINESS WILL COME?
AND JUST WHAT DAY IT'LL BE TAKEN AWAY?

GYPSY BOY, GYPSY BOY,
YOUR EYES REMAIN DRY,
YOU CAN'T EVEN CRY.
YOU'LL READ AND ADVISE
AND NEVER KNOW SURPRISE.
GYPSY BOY, GYPSY BOY,
SO YOUNG TO BE SO WISE.

PICKET FENCE

I LIKE THAT LITTLE PICKET FENCE
YOU PUT AROUND YOUR HEART,
WITH THE PRETTY PINK ROSES,
AND THE THORNS THAT MAKE YOU SMART.

I'VE WALKED AROUND IT QUITE A BIT;
I HAVEN'T FOUND A GATE.
YOU GONNA LET ME IN?
SHOULD I STAY OUT HERE AND WAIT?

LOTS OF PASSERS-BY
COME ALONG YOUR STREET.
"OH," THEY SAY, "LOOK AT THOSE PRETTY ROSES!
AREN'T THEY NEAT?
LOOK AT THAT LITTLE FENCE!
ISN'T THAT SWEET?"

YOU COME OUT TO TIDY UP;
YOU GIVE ME A GREAT BIG SMILE.
YOU SAY HELLO AND WE TALK A LITTLE WHILE.
YOU TREAT ME PRETTY NICE,
THEN YOU GO BACK INSIDE,
AND IT'S LIKE I'VE ONLY SEEN YOU ONCE OR TWICE.

WHEN I TRIED TO CLIMB THAT FENCE
THE THORNS HURT QUITE A LOT.
MY ARMS GOT KIND OF BLOODY,
I PASSED OUT ON THE SPOT.

I REALLY APPRECIATED
THE BAND-AIDS AND THE IODINE.
YOU DRESSED THE WOUNDS SO SWEETLY,
SAID THEY'D HEAL UP FINE.

YOU SURE CAN BE SWEET.
YOU SURE CAN SMILE.
LOOKIN' THROUGH THAT FENCE IS A REAL TREAT.
I COULD DO IT FOR QUITE A WHILE.

I LIKE THAT LITTLE PICKET FENCE
YOU PUT AROUND YOUR HEART,
BUT I'D LIKE TO TAKE A HAMMER
AND SMASH IT ALL APART.

RCA VICTOR
THE SOUND OF MUSIC
LSOD 2005
STEREO

REDECORATION

I SAW YOU FOR A MOMENT
ON THAT BROWN PLAID CHAIR,
THE ONE YOU SAID YOU NEVER LIKED,
BUT I ALWAYS FOUND YOU SITTING THERE.
OF COURSE IT WASN'T YOU,
IT WAS JUST A TRICK OF THE HEART;
I KNOW I'LL NEVER SEE YOU,
THAT WE'RE FOREVER APART.
SO I HAD A GUY COME BY TODAY
IN AN OLD FORD PICK-UP TRUCK;
I HAD HIM HAUL THE CHAIR AWAY,
AND THAT BUREAU WITH THE DRAWER THAT STUCK.
     TIME TO TOSS OUT THE OLD,
     TIME TO BRING IN THE NEW,
     REDECORATE THE HOUSE,
     AND START MY LIFE WITHOUT YOU.
I'VE PAINTED THE BEDROOM ANOTHER COLOR;
IT USED TO BE YOUR FAVORITE BLUE.
NOW IT'S A SORT OF SUNNY YELLOW;
IT CHEERED ME UP WHEN I HAD THE FLU.
THE KITCHEN CABINETS USED TO BE WHITE;
NOW THEY'RE FIRE-ENGINE RED.
I GOT A NEW COFFEE MAKER,
AND TIGER-STRIPED SHEETS FOR THE BED.
     TIME TO TOSS OUT THE OLD,
     TIME TO BRING IN THE NEW,
     REDECORATE THE HOUSE,
     AND START MY LIFE WITHOUT YOU.
I TOOK DOWN THAT MIRROR
AT THE END OF THE UPSTAIRS HALL;
BUILT NEW SHELVES IN THE ATTIC,
BOUGHT NEW CURTAINS AT THE MALL.
I THREW OUT THE PLACEMATS
WITH THE WINE STAINS FROM THAT FIGHT,
GOT RID OF THE WHITE BLANKET
THAT KEPT US WARM AT NIGHT.
YET SOMETIMES WHEN I WAKE
I SEE YOU LYING THERE,
OR SITTING IN THE KITCHEN,
OR WALKING DOWN THE STAIRS.
IT SEEMS I HEAR YOUR VOICE
WHENEVER I ANSWER THE PHONE;
I'VE REDECORATED THE HOUSE,
BUT WHEN WILL YOU LEAVE ME ALONE?
     TIME TO TOSS OUT THE OLD,
     TIME TO BRING IN THE NEW,
     REDECORATE THE HOUSE,
     AND START MY LIFE WITHOUT YOU.

DISGUISE

REMEMBER THAT HALLOWEEN PARTY,
THE ONE GIVEN BY JILL AND MARTY?
THE PILE OF COATS ON THE BED,
THE SWEET THINGS YOU SAID;
LEAVING ON THE MASKS,
REMAINING STRANGERS,
AVOIDING COMPLEXITY
AND PASSION'S DANGERS.
I SAW WHAT OUR LOVE COULD BE
WHEN YOU DIDN'T KNOW IT WAS ME.
SO NOW I'VE STUDIED HARD,
ACQUIRED A BRAND NEW SKILL,
FOUND A NEW WAY
TO WARM UP YOUR CHILL.

I'VE BECOME A MASTER OF DISGUISE,
A WHIZ AT TRANSFORMATION.
WHAT YOU GET
IS NOT NECESSARILY WHAT YOU SEE.
IT JUST MAY BE
THAT EVERY MAN IN YOUR LIFE
IS ME.

SPENT HOURS AT THE GYM
TO BRING YOU BARRY WITH THE ARMS,
AND AFTER THAT, TIM
WITH ALL THOSE PHYSICAL CHARMS.
THE CRASH DIET DIDN'T TAKE LONG:
REMEMBER SENSITIVE ALLAN
WHO PLAYED THE GUITAR
AND WROTE YOU THAT SONG?

FIND YOU'VE BEEN SEEING A LOT OF GUYS?
THAT THEY ALL HAVE PRETTY SIMILAR EYES?
I'M THE MASTER OF DISGUISE,
THE MASTER OF ILLUSION.
YOU THINK YOU SLEEP AROUND A LOT;
IT'S ONLY A DELUSION.
YOU FEEL YOU'RE SO FREE,
BUT, YOU KNOW, IT'S ALWAYS ME.

REMEMBER MIKE EGAN,
THE NEW GUY AT WORK?
WHO YOU ENDED UP THINKING
WAS SUCH A JERK?
BUT THAT WEEK YOU WERE TOGETHER
YOU ALMOST LOST YOUR JOB;
HARDLY GOT OUT OF BED,
JUST LIKE THE WEEK WITH BOB.

REMEMBER DARRYL WITH THE YELLOW CAT,
WHO DROVE YOU CRAZY
THEN LEFT YOU FLAT?
AND EDDIE BECK?
WITH THE BLUE SCORPION
TATTOOED ON HIS NECK?
HE KNEW WHERE TO TOUCH,
AND JUST HOW MUCH.

I REALLY ENJOYED THIS LITTLE GAME,
UNTIL LAST NIGHT, WHEN YOU WHISPERED MY NAME.
YOU WERE SOUND ASLEEP AND LOOKED SO NICE,
YOU KIND OF SIGHED AND SAID IT TWICE.
SO I LEFT YOUR BED IN THE MIDDLE OF THE NIGHT;
SUDDENLY IT JUST DIDN'T SEEM RIGHT.
I GUESS I GOT KIND OF SCARED;
I JUST NEVER KNEW YOU CARED.

THE MASTER OF DISGUISE,
THE MASTER OF ILLUSION.
WAS I REALLY IN DISGUISE,
OR WAS IT JUST MY OWN DELUSION?
I'D HAD A LOT OF FUN,
BUT WAS I FOOLING ANYONE?
NOW THAT MY SCHEME HAS UNFURLED
I THINK IT'S TIME
FOR A TRIP AROUND THE WORLD.

OR CALL 265-
FOR
SALE
GENERAL
GRABBER MT

LINEMAN

AT WORK MY TRUCK IS LIKE MY HOME.
THERE'S MUSIC OF MY CHOICE,
AND SPEED AND WIND AND THE QUIET VOICE
OF VISIONS THAT I DREAD.
THEN EVERY EVENING I COME HOME TO YOU
AND CURL UP ON THE BED.
AT THE EDGE OF THE BLUEST SKY
DISTANT STORM CLOUDS LIE,
AS I, NEXT TO YOU NIGHTLY,
WATCHING YOU SLEEP SO TIGHTLY.
YOUR TRUSTING ARMS
AND YOUR TILTED HEAD
SHOULD MAKE ME FEEL HAPPY,
BUT THEY MAKE ME FEEL SAD INSTEAD.
 I LOVE YOU SO MUCH
 BUT THERE'S A PLACE THAT YOU CAN NEVER TOUCH.
 WHY CAN'T YOU SEE
 THAT YOU'VE ONLY GOT A PART OF ME?
WHY ISN'T THERE A PUZZLE ON YOUR FACE
WHEN I STARE OFF INTO EMPTY SPACE?
DON'T YOU WONDER WHAT I'M THINKING
WHEN I'M LISTENING TO THE BLUES AND DRINKING?
AND DON'T YOU WISH I'D JUST COME HOME TO STAY,
SIT AROUND, WATCH TV AND OCCASIONALLY CLEAN THE FLOOR?
BUT IN MY HEART
THERE ARE DARKER PLACES WHICH I CAN'T IGNORE.
 I LOVE YOU SO MUCH
 BUT THERE'S A PLACE THAT YOU CAN NEVER TOUCH.
 WHY CAN'T YOU SEE
 THAT YOU'VE ONLY GOT A PART OF ME?
 I TRY TO LOVE YOU MORE,
 BUT I FIND IN MY MIND
 DISTANT SPACES WHICH I MUST EXPLORE.
I DON'T WANT TO SEE THE SURPRISE IN YOUR FACE
WHEN YOU WAKE ONE DAY AT DAWN,
LOOK BESIDE YOU AT AN EMPTY PLACE,
AND FIND THAT I HAVE GONE.
THERE'S A SHADOWY LAND
SOMEWHERE IN MY SOUL
OVER WHICH I HAVE NO CONTROL.
 I LOVE YOU SO MUCH
 BUT THERE'S A PLACE THAT YOU CAN NEVER TOUCH.
 WHY CAN'T YOU SEE
 THAT YOU'VE ONLY GOT A PART OF ME?
 WHY CAN'T YOU SEE?

MY TATTOO

I FEEL THE NEED FOR SOMETHING NEW,
LIKE A TATTOO.
IF I DARE
THE QUESTION IS
WHAT?
AND WHERE?

AN ENORMOUS EAGLE ON MY BACK
REACHING FOR THE SUN?
A HEART WITH A SIESMIC CRACK,
A SMALL CHILD HAVING FUN?
CLEOPATRA'S ASP
WRAPPED AROUND MY ARM,
ON MY THIGH A VIEW
OF A WISCONSIN DAIRY FARM?
THE LUCKY NUMBER SEVEN
ON THE PALM OF MY RIGHT HAND,
A FERRIS WHEEL, A CAROUSEL,
THE LOGO OF THE TALKING BAND?
A CHINESE DRAGON,
A BAVARIAN FLAGON,
A PLAYBOY NUDE,
A LIST OF CHINESE FOOD?
A PORTRAIT OF ELVIS
OR JIMMY DEAN,
A ROLLING STONE,
A CORDLESS PHONE,
A BEAUTIFUL SCENE
ON A T.V. SCREEN?

THE BIRTH OF VENUS
RISING ON THE HALF-SHELL,
THE LAST SUPPER,
THE MONA LISA,
THE COLOSSEUM
OR THE TOWER OF PISA?
AN ANCHOR WITH *MA MERE*
ON THE BACK OF MY HAND?
NO. FORGET IRONY OR SATIRE;
NO ONE WILL UNDERSTAND.

A PUMA OR A LEOPARD
ABOUT TO MAKE A KILL,
ANNIE OAKLEY
AND BUFFALO BILL?
AN EGYPTIAN SCARAB
ON MY BACK,
THREE LITTLE KITTENS
IN A GUNNY SACK?

AN EMERALD AND A DIAMOND
TO ADORN MY PRIVATE PARTS,
ACROSS MY CHEST
A CHORUS LINE OF BREAKING HEARTS?
A TIGHTENED NOOSE
TATTOOED 'ROUND MY NECK,
A TRAIN WITH A CABOOSE
ABOUT TO HAVE A WRECK?
THE QUEEN OF HEARTS
OR THE JACK OF SPADES;
OR JUST YOUR NAME:
FIVE LETTERS ACROSS THE KNUCKLES OF MY HAND,
OR A CROWN OF THORNS AS A WEDDING BAND.

I KNOW THAT MY TATTOO WILL BE
A PERMANENT PART OF ME.
THE FLESH MAY LOSE ITS GLOW,
I MAY BE WALKIN' REAL SLOW,
BUT EVEN AFTER THE MORTGAGE IS PAID
MY TATTOO WILL NEVER FADE.
AS YOU REARRANGE MY LIFE
I WANT ONE THING
THAT WILL NEVER CHANGE:
A TATTOO,
IN RED AND BLUE,
SOMETHING ON ME
THAT I CAN ALWAYS SEE;
A TATTOO,
TO REMIND ME
OF YOU.

TIN MAN

TIN MAN, TIN MAN,
YOU FINALLY GOT YOUR HEART.
HOW DOES IT FEEL TO FINALLY FEEL?
HOW DOES IT FEEL TO BE ALMOST REAL?

A HEART'S NOT JUST A TOKEN,
IT'S SOMETHING THAT CAN BE BROKEN.
YOUR METAL-CLAD CHEST COULDN'T PROTECT IT
WHEN YOUR LOVED ONE CAME TO REJECT IT.

TIN MAN, TIN MAN,
YOU FINALLY GOT YOUR HEART.
YOU WANTED IT IN EVERY WAY;
NOW YOU CAN'T EVEN GIVE IT AWAY.

TODAY YOU LOOK SO SHINY AND NEW,
BUT OVER THE YEARS
YOU'LL BE TARNISHED BY YOUR TEARS.
YOUR CAREFREE LIFE HAS FLOWN
NOW THAT YOU KNOW YOU'RE ALONE.

TIN MAN, TIN MAN,
YOU FILLED A VOID WITH A SATIN HEART,
BUT NOW THAT HEART IS EMPTIER
THAN THE VOID WAS AT THE START.
TIN MAN, TIN MAN,
YOU FINALLY GOT YOUR HEART.

RULES OF THE GAME

IS ANYBODY ADDING UP THE POINTS?
IS SOMEBODY KEEPING SCORE?
IS IT ALREADY SEVEN AND FIVE,
OR ONE AND FOUR?

THAT TIME IN HOUSTON I TURNED AWAY FROM YOU
AND REFUSED TO TALK,
WAS THAT BALL FOUR?
DO I HAVE TO TAKE A WALK?

BUT AT SIX FLAGS OVER DALLAS
WHEN I BOUGHT YOU THAT BIRD,
WAS THAT A DOUBLE LETTER,
EVEN A TRIPLE WORD?

IN TULSA WHEN I GOT MAD
AND SLAPPED YOU WITH THE BACK OF MY HAND,
YOU SAID IT DIDN'T HURT,
BUT WAS SOMEONE WATCHING FROM THE STAND?

IN CHICAGO I REMEMBERED,
FOR THE VERY FIRST TIME,
THE EXACT YEAR AND DAY WE MET,
AND THE SODA WE DRANK,
YOU WITH, ME WITHOUT LIME.
SHOULDN'T I GET A POINT OR TWO FOR THAT,
OR AN INSIGNIA TO WEAR ON MY HAT?

I THINK I TRY TO MAKE YOU HAPPY,
TRY TO ALWAYS CARE,
BUT EVERYTIME I FAIL,
DO I HAVE TO GO DIRECTLY TO JAIL?

I HAVEN'T BEEN VERY DECISIVE,
I'VE HAD MY FITS AND STARTS.
DOES A PAIR OF ACES
BEAT MY QUEEN OF HEARTS?

THAT NIGHT AT SPARKIE'S YOU TRIED TO TELL ME
HOW IT FELT TO BE ALONE,
THAT SOMETIMES IT WAS LIKE I WASN'T THERE,
LIKE I DIDN'T CARE.
I LOOKED AT YOU BLANKLY
AND PRETENDED NOT TO UNDERSTAND,
LIKE YOU WERE SPEAKING A LANGUAGE
FROM SOME FOREIGN LAND.
WHAT I REALLY FELT WAS TERROR
AT THE THOUGHT OF LOSING YOU.
WAS THAT A TECHNICAL ERROR?
IS THAT WHY WE'RE THROUGH?

WHAT ARE THE REGULATIONS?
WHAT ARE THE RULES?
WHY DON'T THEY TEACH
THESE THINGS IN SCHOOLS?
WHAT DO I HAVE TO DO
TO SCORE A HOME RUN?
AND IF IT'S A GAME,
SHOULDN'T IT BE FUN?

ON SOME DISTANT JUDGMENT DAY
WILL SOMEBODY LOOK ME IN THE FACE,
POUND A GAVEL AND TELL ME
IF I WON OR LOST THE HUMAN RACE?

evening

MAKE ME YOURS   duet

       GET THAT RED CAT OUT OF THE ATTIC
       PUT THE HEAT ON AUTOMATIC
       CLEAN OUT THE CELLAR
       MAKE ME YOUR FELLER

           PUT YOUR PHOTO IN A LOCKET
           PUT A SKATE KEY IN YOUR POCKET
           BE A PAL
           MAKE ME YOUR GAL

       POUR SOME HONEY IN YOUR DRINK
       WEAR A COAT THAT'S MADE OF MINK
       LEARN HOW TO CRY
       MAKE ME YOUR GUY

           WEAR A BANDANA ON YOUR KNEE
           SAY A PRAYER FOR THE CHESTNUT TREE
           DO SOMETHING SHADY
           MAKE ME YOUR LADY

       PAY ATTENTION TO THE NUMBER FIVE
       SHIFT THAT OLD PACKARD INTO OVERDRIVE
       PUT MUD IN A CAN
       MAKE ME YOUR MAN

           FILL A JAR WITH INDIA INK
           DUMP POTATOES IN THE SINK
           RUN OUT OF MONEY
           MAKE ME YOUR HONEY

               WEAR A MASK TO COVER YOUR FACE
               COME IN FIRST IN A FIVE MILE RACE
               STAY UNDERCOVER
               MAKE ME YOUR LOVER

     SEE CHICAGO ON A BUS
     DRESS UP NICE AND MAKE A FUSS
           TIE A BOX WITH PURPLE STRING
           GO SHOPPING FOR A WEDDING RING
               STAY UP LATE
               MAKE ME YOUR DATE

TAKE A WALK TO THE RACING TRACK
TURN AROUND AND BRING YOURSELF BACK
NEVER SAY HELL
MAKE ME YOUR BELLE

TIE A RIBBON ON YOUR THIGH
FRY AN EGG ON A RAILROAD TIE
PUT ON A SHOW
MAKE ME YOUR BEAU

PUT UP POSTERS IN THE HALL
SEE A MOVIE AT THE MALL
STAND UP REAL SLOW
MAKE ME YOUR DOE

GET SOME MONEY AND PAY YOUR BILLS
GET A GUN AND GO TO THE HILLS
SCRAPE OFF THE MUCK
MAKE ME YOUR BUCK

BUILD A CASTLE IN THE SKY
TEACH AN EAGLE HOW TO FLY
GIVE IN TO FATE
MAKE ME YOUR MATE

YOUR FELLER   YOUR GUY
        YOUR LADY   YOUR GAL
YOUR MAN
        YOUR DOE
                YOUR LOVER.
YOUR BEAU
        YOUR BELLE
                YOUR DATE
YOUR BUCK
        YOUR DOLL
                YOUR MATE

        JUST MAKE ME YOURS
        OKAY?

HARD LOVE

I DON'T THINK I WAS LOOKING
BUT I'M NOT EXACTLY BLIND.
A QUICK HELLO, A DRINK WITH FRIENDS
WAS WHAT I HAD IN MIND.

BUT STARING COLD EYES
IN A FACE NOT YOUNG, NOT OLD
STOPPED ME IN MY TRACKS.
I FELT MY BLOOD RUN COLD.

THE ROOM WAS PRETTY CROWDED
BUT I DID JUST WHAT I PLEASED
I CROSSED THE FLOOR, WENT STRAIGHT TO YOU
AND DROPPED ONTO MY KNEES.

YOU TOOK MY HAIR IN YOUR RIGHT HAND
AND FIRMLY HELD MY HEAD.
YOU KISSED ME HARD UPON THE LIPS
THEN THIS IS WHAT I SAID:

I CAN'T THINK OF ANYTHING
THAT YOU MIGHT WANT TO DO
THAT WOULDN'T BE SOMETHING THAT I WANT
WOULDN'T FEEL GOOD TO ME TOO.
BABY, LET ME BE YOUR SLAVE.

TELL ME WHEN TO STAND AND WHEN TO KNEEL
AND WHEN TO TEAR YOUR NYLON STOCKING SEAM
LIGHT UP THE DARKEST CORNERS OF MY SOUL
WITH YOUR GLARING LASER BEAM

I CAN'T THINK OF ANYTHING
THAT YOU MIGHT WANT TO DO
THAT WOULDN'T BE SOMETHING THAT I WANT
WOULDN'T FEEL GOOD TO ME TOO.
BABY, LET ME BE YOUR SLAVE.

I NEVER THOUGHT OF PAIN BEFORE
AS AN EXTENSION OF DESIRE
I NEVER DREAMED A BED OF LOVE
COULD BE MADE OF ICE AND FIRE.

ON MY CHEST THERE'S NOW A LITTLE MARK
AND A BIGGER GASH ACROSS MY HEART
'CAUSE YOU'VE PLUGGED-IN TO SOMETHING DARK.
I NEVER THOUGHT THIS THING COULD START.

I CAN'T THINK OF ANYTHING
THAT YOU MIGHT WANT TO DO
THAT WOULDN'T BE SOMETHING THAT I WANT
WOULDN'T FEEL GOOD TO ME TOO.
BABY, LET ME BE YOUR SLAVE.

I KNOW THAT I SHOULD RUN FROM YOU
WHILE STRONG AND WHOLE AND WELL
BUT THIS WILL LAST
THE DIE IS CAST
AND HEAVEN'S ONE WITH HELL.

TELL ME WHEN TO STAND AND WHEN TO KNEEL
AND WHEN TO TEAR YOUR NYLON STOCKING SEAM
LIGHT UP THE DARKEST CORNERS OF MY SOUL
WITH YOUR GLARING LASER BEAM.

I CAN'T THINK OF ANYTHING
THAT YOU MIGHT WANT TO DO
THAT WOULDN'T BE SOMETHING THAT I WANT
WOULDN'T FEEL GOOD TO ME TOO.
BABY, LET ME BE YOUR SLAVE.
BABY, BABY, BABY,
LET ME BE YOUR SLAVE.

LOVE JUNKIE

SOMETIMES WHEN WE'RE TOGETHER
YOU LOOK SO HAPPY AND FREE,
THEN I NOTICE
YOU'RE NOT LOOKING AT ME.

I HOLD YOU IN MY ARMS;
I HEAR YOU SAY PLEASE;
IS IT ME YOU NEED,
OR JUST THE SQUEEZE?

FIRST TIME WE GOT IT ON,
ALL DOWN AND FUNKY,
THAT'S WHEN I KNEW
YOU WERE A LOVE JUNKIE.

LOVE JUNKIE,
YOU ALWAYS GIVE A LITTLE SHOVE.
DO YOU NEED ME,
OR DO YOU JUST NEED MY LOVE?

I'M NOT SURE I GOT ENOUGH
OF WHAT YOU HUNGER FOR.
I'M NOT SURE I WANT
TO RUN YOUR CANDY STORE.

YOU ALWAYS TELL ME WHERE TO PUT MY HAND,
AND EXACTLY WHEN TO KISS.
I JUST FOLLOW ORDERS;
IT'S YOU WHO GETS THE BLISS.

LOVE JUNKIE,
I ALWAYS GET A LITTLE SHOVE.
DO YOU NEED ME,
OR DO YOU JUST NEED MY LOVE?

YOU SAY YOU LOVE ME
ALL THE TIME,
BUT IT'S LIKE YOU'RE CONFESSIN'
TO A CRIME.
YOU NEED MY ARMS,
YOU NEED MY LIPS,
YOU NEED MY LOVE,
YOU NEED MY KISS.
I SHOULD HAVE SEEN BEFORE THE START
THAT THERE WERE TRACK MARKS ON YOUR HEART.

LOVE JUNKIE,
YOU ALWAYS GIVE A LITTLE SHOVE.
DO YOU NEED ME,
OR DO YOU JUST NEED MY LOVE?

UES
KER LAMPS
DECORATIONS
RS

SECOND HAND MAN

DO YOU WONDER EVER
WHY QUALITY SEEMS A THING OF THE PAST,
THE THINGS YOU BUY JUST NEVER SEEM TO LAST?
THE HOLE IN THE HEEL
OF THE SOCK YOU HARDLY WORE;
THE SHIRT CUFFS THAT FRAYED
BEFORE YOU EVEN LEFT THE STORE;
THE REFRIGERATOR THAT DOESN'T GET COLD;
THE TELEVISON THAT ALREADY SEEMS OLD.
IF YOU'RE LOOKING FOR VALUE
YOU CAN PROBABLY GET MORE
IF YOU GO TO THE SECOND HAND STORE.
     DO YOU WANT TO BUY A SECOND HAND MAN?
     HE'S CERTAINLY BEEN USED,
     AND A LITTLE ABUSED.
     HIS CORNERS ARE SLIGHTLY WORN.
     HE'S A TINY BIT FRAYED,
     AND SOMEWHAT OVERPLAYED.
     HIS HEART HAS BEEN SLIGHTLY TORN.
     BUT LOOK AT WHAT YOU'VE FOUND:
     A BOOK THAT JUST NEEDS TO BE REBOUND.
     ON SECOND HAND LOVE THERE IS NO BAN.
     WHY DON'T YOU BUY THIS SECOND HAND MAN?
DO YOU WANT TO BUY A SECOND HAND HEART?
IT MAY NOT BE NEWLY MINTED
BUT IT'S TENDER AND IT'S SMART.
THE BOOK'S NOT NEWLY PRINTED
BUT IN IT THERE'S GENUINE ART,
FULL OF THE OLD QUALITY,
HEARTFELT TEARS, AND REAL JOLLITY.
YOU CAN HAVE IT FOR A SONG.
WHY DON'T YOU PACK IT UP AND TAKE IT ALONG?
     DO YOU WANT TO BUY A SECOND HAND MAN?
     HE MAY NOT HAVE FLAWLESS SKIN;
     HE'S TAKEN IT ONCE OR TWICE ON THE CHIN.
     HE'S HAD A BOUT WITH WINE AND GIN;
     HE KNOWS HOW TO LOSE, AND WIN.
     BUT LOOK AT WHAT YOU'VE FOUND:
     A BOOK THAT JUST NEEDS TO BE REBOUND.
     ON SECOND HAND LOVE THERE IS NO BAN.
     WHY DON'T YOU BUY THIS SECOND HAND MAN?
BECAUSE I KNEW WITH JUST ONE GLANCE
THAT NOW I'VE GOT A SECOND CHANCE.
ONE LOOK AT YOU,
I'M AS GOOD AS NEW.
ON SECOND HAND LOVE THERE IS NO BAN.
WHY DON'T YOU BUY THIS SECOND HAND MAN?

PLAIN COOKING

MEETING YOU WAS PRETTY SWELL;
I REMEMBER THOSE DAYS AWFULLY WELL.
YOU BROUGHT ME TO A LOT OF NEW PLACES,
INTRODUCED ME TO A LOT OF NEW FACES,
GAVE ME NEW HORIZONS TO EXPLORE.
YOU OPENED DOORS TO A BIGGER WORLD
THAN I EVER KNEW BEFORE.
YOU SERVED UP AN EXOTIC FABLE
WHENEVER I SAT AT YOUR TABLE.
BUT NOW THAT WE'RE TOGETHER EVERY DAY
THERE'S A COUPLE OF THINGS I'D BETTER SAY:

GIVE ME SOME MASHED POTATOES;
GIVE ME SOME PLAIN WHITE BREAD;
YOU GAVE ME CHOC'LATE TRUFFLES
AND KUMQUATS INSTEAD.
YOU GAVE ME FOREIGN SPICES,
INDULGED IN PECULIAR VICES;
I JUST WANT THE KIND OF FOOD
I REMEMBER AS A CHILD,
NOT THIS STRANGE PROPENSITY
FOR ANYTHING THAT'S WILD.

DID YOU EVER HEAR OF MEAT LOAF?
DID YOU EVER HEAR OF CARROTS?
OF BLUEBERRY COBBLER AND APPLE BROWN BETTY
LIKE USED TO BE BAKED BY MY OLD AUNT NETTIE?
I REMEMBER POT ROAST IN THE OVEN
COOKING REAL SLOW;
PINEAPPLE UPSIDE-DOWN CAKE
IS AS FAR AS I WANT TO GO.

DO YOU HAVE A FRYING PAN?
NO, YOU'VE GOT A WOK.
HOW ABOUT A DOUBLE BOILER?
NO, YOU'VE GOT AN OVEN THAT CAN TALK.
I APPRECIATE ALL THE ATTENTION,
BUT DO YOU MIND IF I MENTION,
I LIKE MY COOKING PLAIN?
HOW OFTEN DO I NEED TO EXPLAIN?

GIVE ME SOME MASHED POTATOES;
GIVE ME SOME PLAIN WHITE BREAD;
YOU GAVE ME ROASTED PHEASANT
AND MANGOES INSTEAD.
YOU GAVE ME FOREIGN SPICES,
INDULGED IN PECULIAR VICES;
I JUST WANT THE KIND OF FOOD
I REMEMBER AS A CHILD,
NOT THIS STRANGE PROPENSITY
FOR ANYTHING THAT'S WILD.

I ADMIT IT'S BEEN AN ADVENTURE;
EXOTIC SPICES SET ME REELING;
THE RED HOT PEPPERS
SENT ME RIGHT UP THROUGH THE CEILING.
BUT I'M LONGING FOR SIMPLER PLEASURES,
LESS EXTREME MEASURES,
ORDINARY TREASURES.

GIVE ME SOME MASHED POTATOES.
GIVE ME SOME PLAIN WHITE BREAD.
YOU GAVE ME MOCHA PASTRIES
AND SNAILS INSTEAD.
YOU GAVE ME FOREIGN SPICES,
INDULGED IN PECULIAR VICES;
I JUST WANT THE KIND OF FOOD
I REMEMBER AS A CHILD;
NOT THIS STRANGE PROPENSITY
FOR ANYTHING THAT'S WILD.

CAN'T YOU JUST CALM DOWN AND BE
JUST A SIMPLE "YOU" TO "ME"?
WITHOUT ALL THIS FANCY COOKERY,
CAN'T WE JUST BECOME A SIMPLE "WE"?

PHONE TALK

HERE I'M SITTING, PHONE IN HAND,
MISSING YOU IN A FAR-OFF LAND.
HI THERE, DARLING, I MISS YOU A LOT.
THE WORK'S OKAY, BUT THE WEATHER'S HOT.

THE DAYS GO SLOW
BUT THE NIGHTS GO SLOWER.
I MISS YOU WHEN IT'S LIGHT,
BUT I MISS YOU MORE
WHEN MY ARMS ARE EMPTY IN THE NIGHT.
I FEEL ALMOST DEAD
IN THIS LUMPY FOREIGN BED.

I'VE BEEN SO ALONE.
BUT NOW I'VE GOT YOU ON THE PHONE
DON'T BE LIKE A HIGH SCHOOL GIRL ALL FLIRTY.
TALK TO ME DIRTY.

DON'T TELL ME 'BOUT THE WEATHER,
OR WHETHER GINNY WET HER BED,
DON'T TELL ME 'BOUT YOUR MOM AND DAD,
OR WHAT LAURA AT THE OFFICE SAID.

I'VE BEEN SO ALONE.
NOW THAT I'VE GOT YOU ON THE PHONE
DON'T HOLD BACK, DON'T BE MEAN,
LET'S BE A LITTLE OBSCENE.

I DON'T THINK OF YOU IN A SENTIMENTAL HAZE,
BUT IN VERY SPECIFIC, CONCRETE WAYS.
I THINK OF THAT SURPRISING SPOT
WHERE THERE'S A LITTLE PATCH OF HAIR.
I THINK ABOUT YOUR ELBOW AND YOUR CHIN,
AND OF ANOTHER PLACE
I'D LIKE TO PUT SOMETHING IN.

I WANT TO KNOW EXACTLY WHAT YOU'RE WEARING,
AND AT JUST WHAT PART OF ME YOU WOULD BE STARING
IF I WAS BY YOUR SIDE.
I WANT TO HEAR THE NAMES OF ALL YOUR PRIVATE PARTS.
I WANT THE FACTS IN SPADES, AND CLUBS, AND HEARTS.
THERE'S NOTHING WE SHOULD HIDE.

ON MA BELL LET'S TURN THE TABLES
AND BURN UP SOME TRANSATLANTIC CABLES.
DON'T BE LIKE A HIGH SCHOOL GIRL ALL FLIRTY.
TALK TO ME DIRTY.

GEMINI MAN

YOU WARNED ME FROM THE START
THAT YOU WOULD BREAK MY HEART.
YOU SAID YOU WERE A GEMINI MAN,
THAT YOU WEREN'T ONE OF THOSE SIMPLE GUYS,
THAT A LOT OF DIFF'RENT PEOPLE
CROWDED THERE BEHIND YOUR EYES.
YOU NEVER TOLD ME ANY LIES,
BUT I DIDN'T REALLY UNDERSTAND
'TILL I HEARD YOU PLAYIN' WITH THE BAND.

I SAW SOMEBODY I NEVER KNEW
WHEN I WAS JUST ALONE WITH YOU.
YET YOUR VOICE AND THE WAY YOU SING
MADE ALL MY BELLS START TO RING.
THE WAY THAT YOU PRONOUNCE YOUR "O"s
PUT THE SUNLIGHT IN MY WINDOWS;
AND WHEN YOU PRONOUNCE YOUR "Z"s
I HEARD THE BUZZIN' OF THE BEES.

GEMINI MAN, GEMINI MAN,
PLAY THAT GUITAR, FAST AS YOU CAN.
FIRST I HEAR YOU SINGIN' PRETTY LOUD,
THEN I WATCH YOU FLIRT WITH THE CROWD.
THE FASTER AND LOUDER THAT YOU PLAY
THE MORE I FEEL YOU DRIFTIN' AWAY.

WHEN YOU SING A SONG THAT ISN'T BLUE
A DEVIL SEEMS TO INHABIT YOU,
BUT HE'S A DEVIL WITH A SMILIN' FACE,
A DEVIL THAT NEVER KNEW DISGRACE.
AND WHEN YOU SING ALL SLOW AND SAD,
WELL, THAT'S A PART OF YOU I NEVER HAD.
YOU GIVE LITTLE WINKS I DON'T UNDERSTAND.
I'M EVEN JEALOUS OF THE GUYS IN THE BAND.

GEMINI MAN, GEMINI MAN,
PLAY THAT GUITAR, FAST AS YOU CAN.
NOW YOU'RE UP UPON THAT STAGE,
SOON YOU'LL BE TOMORROW'S RAGE.
THE FASTER AND LOUDER THAT YOU PLAY
THE MORE I FEEL YOU DRIFTIN' AWAY.

IF THERE WERE REALLY TWO OF YOU
I'D TAKE ONE HOME
AND KEEP IT FOR MY OWN.
THAT OTHER GUY,
PLAYIN' WITH THE BAND,
HE'LL JUST NEVER UNDERSTAND.

GEMINI MAN, GEMINI MAN,
PLAY THAT GUITAR, FAST AS YOU CAN.
NOW YOU'RE UP UPON THAT STAGE,
SOON YOU'LL BE TOMORROW'S RAGE.
THE FASTER AND LOUDER THAT YOU PLAY
THE MORE I FEEL YOU DRIFTIN' AWAY.

GEMINI MAN, GEMINI MAN,
I'LL ALWAYS BE YOUR BIGGEST FAN;
BUT NOW I SEE WHY NOBODY CAN
HOLD THE LOVE OF A GEMINI MAN.

TELL ME

CAN IT BE TRUE
THERE'S NOTHING I CAN DO
TO MAKE YOU FEEL ABOUT ME
THE WAY I FEEL ABOUT YOU?
NO BUTTONS I CAN PUSH?
NO MEDALS I CAN EARN?
NO FENCES I CAN MEND?
NO BRIDGES I CAN BURN?
TELL ME.
CAN THERE REALLY BE NOTHING?
NO WAY?
TELL ME SOMETHING, ANYTHING,
I'LL DO IT TODAY.
TELL ME.
I'LL HELP YOU MOVE THE REFRIGERATOR;
I'LL SCRUB YOUR KITCHEN FLOOR;
TAKE OUT ALL YOUR GARBAGE;
FIX THE SQUEAK IN YOUR BATHROOM DOOR.
TELL ME,
SHOULD I DO SOMETHING FOOLISH AND WILD,
OR SOMETHING CALM AND WISE?
SHOULD I THROW OUT ALL MY CLOTHES,
OR CHANGE THE COLOR OF MY EYES?
TELL ME.

I REALLY DO LOVE YOU;
I WANT YOU TO LOVE ME TOO.
WHY DON'T YOU JUST TELL ME
WHAT I'VE GOT TO DO?
TELL ME.
PLEASE, TELL ME.

THE JUNGLE

MY HEART'S A JUNGLE
A DEADLY SNARE
PAY A VISIT
IF YOU DARE

YOU'LL HEAR WILD CRIES
IN THE BLACKNESS OF NIGHT
YOU WON'T GET OUT
WITHOUT A FIGHT

IT'S CLOSE AND HOT
IN THIS SPELLBOUND PLACE
THERE'S WILD CREATURES
FLYING 'ROUND YOUR FACE

THERE'RE DARK PLACES
AND TANGLED VINES
MYSTERIOUS SPACES
AND DIAMOND MINES

A PANTHER IN THE TREE ABOVE
A PYTHON 'ROUND YOUR THROAT
ONE LITTLE SQUEEZE
THAT'S ALL SHE WROTE

IT'S EVERYTHING YOU FEAR
IT'S EVERYTHING YOU DREAD
BUT TAKE A STEP, DRAW NEAR
FORGET THE THINGS YOU SAID

I SEE THE PANIC
AS YOU LOOK IN MY EYES
BUT OVERCOME YOUR TERROR
HERE ENCHANTMENT LIES

MY HEART'S A JUNGLE
A PAGAN RITE
YOU'VE HEARD THE BARK
NOW-- TRY THE BITE

night

TWO WHITE DOORS

I REMEMBER AS A KIND OF HEAVEN
THE HOUSE IN WHICH I LIVED
WHEN I WAS SIX OR SEVEN,
AND THE ROOM I SLEPT IN EVERY NIGHT;
MOM TUCKED ME IN AND SAID "SLEEP TIGHT,"
AND SOMETIMES LAUGHED AND ADDED,
"DON'T LET THE BED-BUGS BITE."

TWO WHITE DOORS... TWO WHITE DOORS...

THAT ROOM HAS TWO WHITE DOORS;
ONE LEADS THROUGH THE HALL
TO A WORLD IN WHICH I CAN'T COMPETE,
GAMES I CANNOT PLAY,
VEGETABLES I HAVE TO EAT;
THE OTHER TO A SMALLER ROOM
WHERE SUMMER CLOTHES GO IN THE FALL,
QUILTED BAGS FILLED WITH COATS,
BOXES OF FORGOTTEN TOYS, SHOES AND BOOTS,
FANCY DRESSES AND GROWN-UP SUITS.
INSIDE THAT SECRET PLACE
I PUT MY HANDS ACROSS MY FACE
AND LET MY MIND ROAM FREE;
I CAN BE WHATEVER I WANT TO BE.

SOARING TO THE FORTIETH FLOOR
IN AN ELEVATOR TO THE SKY,
I CAN EXPLORE OTHER PLANETS,
I CAN FLY.
I INVENT MASTER RACES
BY MAKING FUNNY FACES,
AND BURY PIRATE TREASURE
IN CAVERNS WITHOUT MEASURE.

IN MY SPACE-AGE KITCHEN
I TURN OUT PIES AND CAKES;
I FEED THE HUNGRY OF THE WORLD;
I KNOW WHAT IT TAKES.
WHEN I'M A SKILLFUL SURGEON
I DON'T USE REAL KNIVES,
BUT I NEVER LOSE A PATIENT;
I SAVE A LOT OF LIVES.

I GIVE SOME MILD LASHINGS
IN A DUNGEON DEEP;
I FEEL THE PULL OF MUSCLES IN MY BACK
WHEN I'M STRETCHED ACROSS A MEDIEVAL RACK.
IN ELABORATE DISGUISE
I RESCUE A HOSTAGE TIED TO A TREE;
LEAD THROUGH A DISMAL SWAMP
A BEAUTIFUL MAIDEN WHO CANNOT SEE.

TWO WHITE DOORS... TWO WHITE DOORS...

THE MOONLIGHT OFTEN MADE A GLOW
ON THOSE DOORS I STARED AT EVERY NIGHT;
BEHIND ONE THE REAL WORLD,
BEHIND THE OTHER, DELIGHT.
THERE I WAS ABLE TO DREAM AND EXPLORE;
HENCE THE CURRENT USAGE I DEPLORE:
AS A PRIVATE PLACE WHERE BATTLES ARE WON
A CLOSET CAN BE A LOT OF FUN.

LONG ISLAND

IT'S SUMMER AND THE WORK WEEK ENDS.
I'M HEADED OUT TO MONTAUK TO SPEND A DAY WITH FRIENDS.
A RENTED CAR, SOME TAPES FROM HOME,
NO ONE CAN REACH ME ON THE PHONE.
I'M OUT OF THE CITY BEFORE THE SUN COMES UP;
I EAT A BAGEL AND DRINK A CUP OF DECAF LIGHT.
I FEEL THE LINES ON MY FOREHEAD ERASE
AS THE MORNING LIGHT STREAMS ACROSS MY FACE.
WHEN YOU THINK, IT'S KIND OF FUNNY,
ALL THE THINGS WE HAVE TO DO FOR MONEY.
        LIFE IS HAPPY, LIFE IS SAD;
        IT MIXES UP THE GOOD AND BAD,
        THE NOBLE AND THE CHEAT,
        THE BITTER AND THE SWEET.

THERE ARE CARS OF FAMILIES AND PEOPLE IN PAIRS,
I'M LOOKING FORWARD TO A DAY WITHOUT CARES;
BUT JUST BEFORE EXIT FIFTY-THREE
THERE'S SOMETHING MORE COMPLEX WAITING FOR ME.
DARK ROOFS AND A TOWER RISE BEYOND THE HILLS;
I THINK OF BLAKE'S SATANIC MILLS.
IT'S A PLACE FOR THOSE WHO CANNOT COPE,
A PLACE FOR THOSE WHO'VE LOST THEIR HOPE.
I THINK OF A SISTER THAT I ONCE HAD,
WHOSE GOOD TIMES WERE OUTNUMBERED BY BAD.
        LIFE IS HAPPY, LIFE IS SAD;
        IT MIXES UP THE GOOD AND BAD,
        THE SWEET AND THE SOUR,
        THE MOMENT AND THE HOUR.

AT SIXTY MILES-AN-HOUR THE SCENERY CHANGES QUICKLY NOW,
AND BEFORE I KNOW I'M SITTING ON THE BOW.
THERE'S BAIT AND BEER, THE SUN IS LIKE A SILVER SPEAR;
THE BLUES ARE RUNNING AND THE SKY IS CLEAR,
BUT THERE'S A VISION HAUNTING ME:
A TEMPLE OF MISERY BY THE L.I.E.
        LIFE IS HAPPY, LIFE IS SAD;
        IT MIXES UP THE GOOD AND BAD,
        THE SNEAKY AND THE TRUE,
        THE ROTTEN AND THE NEW,
        THE REAL AND THE SHAM,
        THE SERPENT AND THE LAMB,
        AS THE MINUTES AND THE DAYS
        DISSOLVE INTO A DISTANT HAZE.

LEAVE A PLACE FOR ME

YOU'VE MOVED AWAY
TO ANOTHER HOUSE,
A MANSION ACROSS THE WAY
WITH ROLLING LAWNS AND BIG GREEN TREES,
FOREIGN CARS IN THE DRIVE.
IT'S WHAT YOU WANT, YOU SAY,
IT MAKES YOU FEEL ALIVE.

IN THE NEW LIFE YOU FOUND
YOU'LL ORDER SERVANTS AROUND,
ACSCEND MARBLE STAIRS,
BE PUTTING ON AIRS,
BUT REMEMBER TURNING ON THE LIGHTS AT THREE A.M.,
REMEMBER THAT BIRTHMARK ON MY KNEE,
REMEMBER TWO-DAY-OLD COFFEE,
REMEMBER WHERE YOU GOT STUNG BY A BEE,
AND LEAVE THE BACK DOOR OPEN,
LEAVE A PLACE FOR ME.

I'LL MEET YOU UNDER THE BASEMENT STAIRS,
BEHIND THE FURNACE IF YOU DARE;
YOU'LL GET A LITTLE DIRTY,
BUT YOU NEVER USED TO CARE.
WE'LL DO JUST LIKE WE DID BEFORE
WHEN WE USED A MAGIC MARKER
AND KEPT SCORE ON THE WOODEN FLOOR;
SO REMEMBER,
DON'T LOCK UP THE CELLAR DOOR.

YOU'LL SLEEP ON SATIN SHEETS,
BRUSH YOUR TEETH IN CRYSTAL LIGHT,
BE CALM AND CIVILIZED,
NEVER HAVE A FIGHT;
BUT I'LL BE THERE
IN THAT LITTLE ROOM YOU ONCE CALLED HOME;
I WON'T GO FAR,
MAYBE DRINKING AT THE KOZY KORNER BAR;
SO DON'T FORGET
TO LEAVE THE BASEMENT DOOR AJAR.

WHEN YOU'VE FINISHED DINING,
OR AFTER A FORMAL BALL,
YOU MAY HEAR A SINGLE RING
FROM THE PHONE THAT'S IN THE HALL;
IT'S MY CALL.
EDDIE AND BAGS WON'T BARK;
THEY KNOW A FRIEND.
YOU CAN DEPEND ON ME, YOU'LL SEE:
JUST LEAVE THE BACK DOOR OPEN,
LEAVE A PLACE FOR ME.

IN THE NIGHT

HAD A FRIGHT
WOKE UP IN THE NIGHT
SWEAT ON THE PILLOW
BLOOD ON THE STAIR
EVERYTHING WAS DIFF'RENT
YOU WEREN'T THERE

IN THE BATHROOM
THE TUB HAD OVERFLOWED
THE MIRROR BECAME A TOMB
MY EYES, THEY KINDA GLOWED

THUNDER IN THE SKY
LIGHTNING IN THE HALL
PILLOWS BEGAN TO FLY
I WAS FEELIN' STRANGELY TALL

CHAIRS BEGAN TO DANCE
SHEETS BEGAN TO TEAR
SOON THERE WAS POPCORN
WHIZZING THROUGH THE AIR

THE GHOST OF ELVIS
WAS SITTING ON A SWING
THE ROOM STARTED SPINNIN'
WHEN HE BEGAN TO SING

FIFTY DOORS OF DIFF'RENT COLORS
EACH ONE WITH A LOCK
FIFTY BROKEN WINDOWS
HANDS WITHOUT A CLOCK

I HEARD YOUR VOICE
DOWN EVERY HALL
HAD TO MAKE A CHOICE
HAD TO MAKE THE CALL

A DOZEN RIFLES AT MY HEAD
A SILENCE... A SHOT...
I WOKE, I WASN'T DEAD
AND THERE YOU WERE
SLEEPIN' IN THE BED
I HELD YOU TIGHT
YOU OPENED YOUR EYES
"BABY, SORRY FOR THE FIGHT
SORRY FOR THE LIES"
YOU SMILED, KISSED ME
SAID "LET IT BE"
WE SLEPT PRETTY TIGHT
THE REST OF THE NIGHT

Edited by BOB SEALY
Designed by DAVID STEKERT

All photographs taken by Fred Kolo on Eastern Long Island.

Special thanks to Mary Liz Kemmerer, Bob Sealy, David Stekert,
Linda Skipper, Karena Fowler, James Loehlin, and Kriss Roebling.

Printed by Thomson-Shore, Dexter, Michigan U.S.A.

COLUMBINE PRESS,
P.O. Box 363
East Hampton, NY 11937
SAN 298-8194

ADDITIONAL COPIES OF HEART BEATS may be ordered at
$12.00 per copy plus $2.00 postage and handling charge.
New York state residents please add sales tax.
Send check or money order to:
  Columbine Press
  P O Box 363 A
  East Hampton NY 11937
Please include name, mailing address with zip code and
daytime telephone number.